AF344807

The Architect of Possibilities

How Visionaries and Entrepreneurs Build Game-Changing Businesses and Industries

JUSTINE EHIWARIO

TABLE OF CONTENTS

Copyright © 2025 Justine Ehiwario

All rights reserved.

SUMMARY

THE ARCHITECT OF POSSIBILITIES

How Visionaries and Entrepreneurs Build Game-Changing Businesses and Industries

By Justine Ehiwario

Are you ready to build something that truly matters?

In The Architect of Possibilities, Justine Ehiwario—renowned entrepreneur, engineer, and author of The Unstoppable Road to Wealth Creation and The Mind of a Trillionaire—offers a master blueprint for turning bold visions into transformative businesses. This book is not just about entrepreneurship; it's about legacy, impact, and the courage to create what the world has never seen.

With a rare blend of strategic insight and real-world application, Justine shows how to:

- Think like a visionary and lead like a builder
- Design business models that solve real-world problems
- Build a resilient team and culture that thrives on innovation
- Navigate crisis, competition, and market disruption with clarity
- Scale your operations without losing your soul or values
- Fund long-term growth with strategic capital

Drawing from personal experience across industries—including fashion (JAY T CLOTHING), tech (Justech International), real estate (Jay T Prime Properties & Jay T Luxury Homes), and engineering—Justine combines inspiration, practical wisdom, and powerful storytelling.

If you're ready to go beyond business-as-usual and build something timeless, this book is your roadmap.

Book Summary – The Blueprint in Brief

Core Thesis:

Visionary entrepreneurs are not merely business builders—they are architects of the future. They imagine boldly, design intentionally, and build structures—companies, products, cultures, systems—that transform industries and uplift humanity.

Key Themes:

- Bold vision and practical execution are not opposites—they are partners.
- Culture is as critical as code, products, or profit.
- Leadership evolves as companies scale.
- Creativity is a strategic asset—not a side effect.
- Long-term growth requires strategic capital, systems thinking, and resilient leadership.

Final Takeaway:

This book is more than theory. It is a toolkit for builders who are willing to shape the next decade with courage, creativity, and commitment. Whether you're starting small or scaling globally, you are not just building a business—you are architecting possibility.

What you build can change everything.

DISCLAIMER

The information contained in this book, *The Architect of Possibilities: How Visionaries and Entrepreneurs Build Game-Changing Businesses and Industries*, is provided for educational and inspirational purposes only. While every effort has been made to ensure the accuracy and reliability of the content, the author, Justine Ehiwario, and the publisher disclaim any liability for any losses or damages that may arise directly or indirectly from the use or application of the information provided.

This book does not constitute legal, financial, or professional advice. Readers are encouraged to consult with qualified professionals before making any business, investment, or legal decisions.

Any examples, case studies, or scenarios presented in this book are for illustrative purposes only and do not guarantee similar results.

The author's opinions and views expressed in this book are personal and may evolve over time.

By reading this book, you agree to hold the author and publisher harmless from any claims or liabilities arising from your use of the information contained herein.

Introduction:

The Architect of Possibilities:

How Visionaries and Entrepreneurs Build Game-Changing Businesses and Industries.

The Blueprint of Destiny

"The future belongs to those who see possibilities before they become obvious."

— *The Architect of Possibilities*

The World Wasn't Built by Doubters

Look around you—the phone in your hand, the skyscrapers scraping the sky, the electric car humming silently through traffic—none of these were built by doubters. They were crafted by architects of possibility. Men and women who had the audacity to believe that the world wasn't finished yet. That something better could be built. That the status quo could be disrupted, redesigned, and redefined.

This book is not for the faint-hearted. It is for the visionaries, the pioneers, the dreamers who don't just wait for the future—they build it. Whether you're a startup founder trying to crack a code, a leader inside a massive corporation fighting inertia, or someone with a burning idea they've kept quiet for too long—this book is your blueprint.

Let's get to work.

Possibility is the New Currency

In today's world, the most valuable commodity isn't oil, gold, or even data. It's **possibility**. The ability to see what others can't. To imagine solutions to problems the world hasn't solved yet. To bring into existence something that once lived only in the imagination.

Possibility-thinking is what made Elon Musk launch rockets into space without government backing. It's what turned a college dorm project into Facebook. It's how Airbnb and Uber disrupted decades-old industries. These weren't lucky breaks. They were built from bold ideas, clear vision, and relentless execution.

The power to create—really create—is no longer reserved for a select few with inherited wealth or elite connections. In this age of accelerated information, global communication, and decentralized platforms, anyone with a vision and the courage to execute can build something extraordinary.

That includes you.

From Vision to Execution

Every great business or industry-altering idea starts the same way: as a **vision**. A spark. A whisper of what could be. But vision alone isn't enough. There must be structure. A foundation. A framework to build from. That's where the **architect** comes in.

An architect doesn't merely dream. An architect draws. Designs. Constructs. Tests. Adjusts. Rebuilds. An architect turns the invisible into the visible.

This book will show you how to go from abstract vision to concrete reality. From inspiration to innovation. From potential to performance.

We'll explore what sets world-class visionaries and entrepreneurs apart—not just in terms of what they do, but how they think, how they build, and how they adapt.

The Machinery of Disruption

Disruption is no longer a buzzword—it's a *blueprint*. The most successful companies and innovators of our time didn't just compete. They *rewrote the rules*.

Netflix didn't just make better movies—it redefined entertainment. Amazon didn't just build a store—it reinvented the supply chain. Canva didn't just improve graphic design—it democratized it.

In each of these cases, someone dared to ask: "What if there's a better way?"

This book will dive into that question—not with theoretical fluff, but with real frameworks, case studies, and principles used by the builders of modern-day empires.

You'll learn what fuels disruption, how to identify market gaps, and how to stay ahead in an environment where change is not just constant—it's accelerating.

Vision is Not Enough

Many people have great ideas. Fewer execute. Fewer still build legacies. The graveyard of failed startups is filled with "great ideas" that never became great businesses.

The difference lies in **execution**. This book will teach you how to operationalize your vision. How to build systems that scale. How to attract top talent, raise capital, and lead with clarity.

More importantly, you'll learn the inner architecture—the mindset—of people who don't fold under pressure, who learn from failure, and who turn every setback into a setup for something greater.

Building with Purpose

True architects of possibility don't build *just to build*. They create with intention. They build with impact in mind. They ask themselves not just "What can I do?" but "What should I do?" and "How will it serve the world?"

Game-changing entrepreneurs are not just chasing profits. They're chasing purpose. They're creating new ecosystems. Solving real problems. Shifting entire cultures.

You'll learn how to align your vision with a mission bigger than yourself—and why doing so isn't just noble, but strategic. Purpose gives clarity. It gives direction. And it keeps you going when everything else screams, "Quit."

The Architect's Mindset

This book will challenge the way you think. That's intentional.

You cannot build a new reality with old patterns. The thinking that got you here won't take you there. You need mental models for innovation. You need clarity. You need resilience. You need what I call the **Architect's Mindset**— a fusion of vision, strategy, creativity, and grit.

Throughout this journey, I'll walk you through how to develop this mindset, nurture it, and use it to navigate the chaos of modern entrepreneurship.

What You'll Learn in This Book

Here's a glimpse of what we'll cover in the chapters ahead:

1. **How visionaries see opportunities others miss**
2. **The psychology of world-class entrepreneurs**
3. **Designing solutions that scale**
4. **Failing forward and building resilience**
5. **The mechanics of innovation and disruption**
6. **Building teams, culture, and legacy**
7. **Turning your possibility into a movement**

Each chapter will end with a practical framework you can use immediately to apply what you've learned—whether you're starting out, scaling, or pivoting.

Why I Wrote This Book

I wrote this book because I've seen what happens when potential goes unrealized. I've seen brilliant ideas die in silence. I've watched people shrink their dreams to fit their fears. And I've seen others—no smarter, no more gifted—build empires because they believed it was possible.

My mission is simple: **to ignite the architect within you**. To equip you with the tools, the mindset, and the fire to build something that matters.

Because the world doesn't need more copycats. It needs creators. Builders. Possibility architects.

It needs *you*.

Chapter 1:

Chapter 1: The Possibility Blueprint

"Before you build the business, build the blueprint. Before you scale the dream, scale the belief."
— *Justine Ehiwario*

The Architect Begins with Belief

No nation, movement, enterprise, or dynasty was ever built by accident. Every great company and industry you admire today was once an invisible reality that existed only in the imagination of someone bold enough to believe.

In *The Things Wealthy People Do*, I said:
"The difference between the dreamers and the builders is this—builders believe enough to begin."

What separates high-achievers and visionary entrepreneurs from the rest is not access to capital, perfect timing, or connections—it's their **internal architecture**. The **possibility blueprint** is that internal structure. It's where creativity meets conviction. It's the mental framework that turns ordinary minds into legendary forces.

Seeing What Others Overlook

Visionaries aren't lucky—they're trained to see what others ignore.

In *The Mind of a Trillionaire*, I wrote:

"Wealth doesn't first appear in bank accounts. It appears in the depth of imagination, then in the decisions that follow."

A builder sees gaps and responds with solutions. Where others see an empty lot, the builder envisions a skyline.

Scenario: From Waste to Wealth

In Ghana, two brothers began collecting waste plastic bottles from the streets. People mocked them, laughed at their dream of turning trash into treasure. Today, their company **Nelplast Eco Ghana** turns plastic waste into strong, eco-friendly building materials and employs over 300 people.

They didn't just see plastic—they saw potential. Their blueprint wasn't paper—it was **possibility**.

Core Pillars of the Possibility Blueprint

To build something remarkable, your possibility blueprint must be anchored on **five unshakable foundations**:

1. A Problem Worth Solving

Every great business begins by solving a specific problem. If you can't define the problem clearly, you cannot offer a relevant solution. As I said in *The Unstoppable Road to Wealth Creation*:

"The problem is the platform. Stand on it, not under it."

2. A Solution With Soul

Your idea must carry emotional weight. It must resonate, touch lives, and stir purpose. When your solution feels meaningful to people, it becomes unforgettable—and unstoppable.

3. A Map, Not Just a Mission

Every architect needs a map. Vision without a structure is chaos in disguise. The blueprint includes timelines, projections, frameworks, key partnerships, and execution strategies.

4. A Community of Belief

Your idea can't grow in isolation. You must surround yourself with those who feed your faith—not your fears. Builders need builders.

5. A Resilient Spirit

Rejection, doubt, and delays are part of the building process. If you quit after a "no," you weren't building—just testing. Resilience is your greatest raw material.

Building Begins Where Fear Ends

Too many dreams die at the door of fear. Fear of failure. Fear of being mocked. Fear of wasting time.

But here's the truth:

"Every blueprint requires risk before it can rise." — Justine Ehiwario

Do you think Jeff Bezos was certain Amazon would dominate? No. But he had clarity on one thing: that customer convenience in the digital age was the future. That clarity was enough for him to begin in a garage.

You don't need every answer. You need **enough clarity to take the next bold step**.

Practical Framework: Designing Your Possibility Blueprint

Let's walk through a framework you can begin applying today:

Blueprint Worksheet – Answer These Deeply:

1. **The Vision**: What do I feel deeply called to build?
2. **The Burden**: What problem or injustice won't leave me alone?
3. **The Advantage**: What do I know, own, or do that could give me a unique edge?
4. **The Proof**: Have I seen this possibility demonstrated—even in a small way?
5. **The Obstacle**: What is stopping me right now?
6. **The Next Action**: What small step can I take in the next 24 hours?

Possibility, Not Perfection

You do not need a perfect plan—you need a possibility worth pursuing. Perfection stalls motion. Possibility invites action.

Consider this:

"If your dream doesn't scare you, it's probably not from your future."

What you're being called to build won't always be logical—it will stretch you. It'll demand more wisdom, courage, and sacrifice than you feel prepared to give.

But the stretching is the shaping.

Case Study: Canva – A Blueprint in Action

Melanie Perkins started teaching graphic design at her university. She noticed how difficult design tools like Photoshop were for non-designers. That was the *problem*. Her *solution*? Build a drag-and-drop design tool accessible to everyone.

She sketched her idea in notebooks. No capital. No team. Just a conviction that design should be universal.

Today, **Canva** is valued over **$40 billion**, serving over 100 million users globally.

All because she didn't just see a problem—she built the possibility blueprint to solve it.

Journal Prompt – Activate Your Architect's Mind

Close your eyes and imagine it's 10 years from now. You've built what you dream of today. What does it look like? Who did it help? What changed because of your courage to begin? Now write it all down in detail.

The Mindset of the Builder

Your mindset is your master tool. As I wrote in *The DNA of Financial Greatness*: *"You can't build a mansion with a shack mentality. Upgrade your mind and the results will match."*

Think like a builder. Move like a founder. Speak like a CEO. Plan like an architect. Act like it's already possible—because it is.

Final Word: Don't Wait—Draw

You don't need permission to begin. You don't need a loan to draw the first sketch. You don't need approval to think big. You are the architect of your possibility. And this chapter—this moment—is your foundation.

So draw. Design. Dream. Decide.

Your blueprint is waiting. And so is the world.

Justine Ehiwario

Chapter 2:

Visioneering – Designing the Future from the Inside Out

"Where there is no vision, businesses perish. Where vision is clear, strategy becomes unstoppable."
— Justine Ehiwario

What Is Visioneering?

Visioneering is the process of mentally engineering your future before it physically exists. It is not daydreaming. It is deliberate. It is dynamic. It is the blueprint of the future etched in faith, strategy, and creativity.

In *The Mind of a Trillionaire,* I described vision as: *"The mental construction site where all great futures are built long before reality catches up."*

Every builder of possibilities begins by **seeing** what isn't yet visible.

Vision vs Sight

There's a fundamental difference between **sight** and **vision**:

- **Sight** is limited to the eyes.

- **Vision** is fueled by insight, foresight, and divine alignment.

Helen Keller once said,

"The only thing worse than being blind is having sight but no vision."

You can't lead a business, a team, or an industry with sight alone. It requires a deeper dimension of seeing.

Vision Is Specific, Not Vague

You're not called to build something *general*. Visionaries aren't vague—they're sharp.

"If you can't define your vision in one sentence, you don't own it yet."
— *Justine Ehiwario, The Things Wealthy People Do*

Let's look at some sharp, world-shaping visions:

- **Tesla (Elon Musk):** *"To accelerate the world's transition to sustainable energy."*
- **Airbnb:** *"To create a world where anyone can belong anywhere."*
- **Jay T Prime Properties:** *"To design wealth through real estate innovation and excellence."*

The more refined your vision, the easier it is to:

- Attract resources
- Mobilize people
- Design strategy
- Sustain momentum

The Visioneering Process

Here's a step-by-step framework to engineer your vision into existence:

1. Capture the Calling

Ask: *What is deeply pulling at my spirit to build or solve?*

Every vision starts with a burden. An unrest. A spark that won't go away. This isn't random—it's a clue.

2. Craft the Clarity

Write it down. Rework it until it's memorable. Your vision statement should be:

- Short
- Strong
- Specific

Example:

"To end energy poverty in Africa through affordable solar

technology."

Now that's a vision that inspires investment and action.

3. Visualize the Impact

What does your vision look like **when it succeeds**?

- How many people are affected?
- What legacy does it leave?
- What change does it create?

4. Engineer Backward

Start from the end and reverse-engineer the steps required. Work backwards from your future.

Case Study: The Rise of Spanx – Vision Born from Frustration

Sara Blakely couldn't find undergarments that gave her the look she wanted in white pants. She didn't just complain—she **visioneered** a solution. With $5,000, she designed the first prototype for **Spanx**.

She had never been in fashion. No investors. No background.

But she had vision. That was her advantage.

Today, Spanx is a billion-dollar company. Sara became the youngest self-made female billionaire.

Lesson? The pain you feel may be the portal to the possibility you're called to build.

The Power of Vision-Driven Execution

In *The Unstoppable Road to Wealth Creation*, I emphasized: *"Ideas don't build empires—executed vision does."*

Vision must move from paper to product, from idea to institution. But that movement requires:

- **Strategic focus**
- **Clear milestones**
- **Courage to start before everything is perfect**

Visioneering Tools – A Quick Toolkit

Here are practical tools to help solidify your vision:

Tool	Purpose
Vision Board	Use images, words, and timelines to create a visual of your future.
Vision Script	Write a 1-2 page detailed story of your business 5 years from now.
Founder's Manifesto	A bold declaration of what you stand for and will never compromise.
Vision Tracker	Weekly check-ins on alignment, progress, and pivots.

Inspirational Quote

"Everything visible today was once invisible until someone dared to believe."

— Justine Ehiwario, The DNA of Financial Greatness

Journal Exercise

- What is my exact vision? (Write in one sentence)
- Who will benefit the most from this vision?
- What does success look like in 10 years?

Write it. Declare it. Visualize it daily.

Final Thoughts: Lead with Light

Vision is not optional—it's your north star.

Without it, strategy becomes guesswork. With it, even your smallest steps gain momentum.

As you continue building your enterprise or legacy, remember: **you are not following a path—you are creating one**. And vision is your compass.

Justine Ehiwario

Chapter 3:

Possibility Teams – Building With Giants, Not Just Hands

"If you want to go fast, go alone. If you want to go far and build the future, build with giants."
— *Justine Ehiwario*

Why You Need a Possibility Team

No visionary builds an empire alone. Behind every revolutionary company is a team of **giants**—people who think beyond limits, stretch boundaries, and carry the vision with the same fire as the founder.

In *The Things Wealthy People Do*, I wrote:
"The quality of your outcomes is often a reflection of the caliber of your associations."

A Possibility Team is not just a group of professionals you hire. It is a collection of minds who share your hunger to birth something exceptional. They are aligned in purpose, fueled by shared belief, and committed to the mission.

What Makes a Team a "Possibility Team"?

A Possibility Team is different from a regular team. Here's what sets them apart:

Quality	Regular Team	Possibility Team
Mindset	Task-focused	Mission-driven
Engagement	Passive	Passionate
Skillset	Competent	Constantly growing
Alignment	Working for a paycheck	Working for a purpose
Vision clarity	Follows instructions	Takes initiative to grow the vision

They don't just execute — they **expand**.

7 Essential Pillars of a Possibility Team

1. Shared Vision

Every member must know the vision, see it clearly, and understand their role in its execution.

Example:

When Steve Jobs built Apple, he didn't just hire engineers—he gathered evangelists who saw computing as a way to **empower humanity**.

2. Trust Culture

Trust is the foundation. In *The DNA of Financial Greatness*, I noted that:

"Trust is the currency of leadership; once spent recklessly, rebuilding it becomes expensive."

Possibility Teams must trust the leader, the process, and each other.

3. High Ownership Mentality

They don't wait for instructions. They see problems and proactively build solutions.

4. Excellence Standard

Good enough is never enough. Mediocrity is rejected at all levels. They strive for exceptionalism.

5. Strategic Diversity

Different skills, experiences, and perspectives fuel innovation. A great team is not uniform — it's **unified in mission, diverse in function**.

6. Emotional Intelligence

They know how to manage conflict, understand people, and respond to challenges with maturity.

7. Continual Growth

They learn, unlearn, and relearn. They evolve with the vision.

Case Study: How Elon Musk Builds Possibility Teams

Elon Musk doesn't build companies the traditional way. He assembles teams around **impossible missions**—like colonizing Mars or building fully autonomous electric vehicles.

He prioritizes:

- First-principles thinkers
- Obsession with the mission
- Ability to handle extreme pressure

He once said:

"I don't care where you went to school. If you've solved tough problems, I want to talk to you."

His hiring philosophy reveals something powerful: **Great teams are built around great questions, not just great resumes.**

How to Build Your Possibility Team

Here's a practical roadmap to attract and lead your own team of vision-driven collaborators:

1. Define the Mission Clearly

People want to follow purpose, not just plans. Craft a powerful mission statement and communicate it daily.

2. Hire for Mindset First

Skills can be taught. Hunger, grit, and imagination cannot.

3. Create Ownership Structures

Give them stakes in the mission. Let them feel like partners, not passengers.

4. Cultivate a Culture of Possibility

Celebrate experimentation. Encourage big thinking. Normalize calculated risk.

5. Offer Growth Paths

The best talent is hungry for growth. Build systems where they grow personally and professionally as the company grows.

6. Model the Standard

You are the thermostat. Whatever standard you uphold becomes the team's climate.

The Possibility Roles You Need Early On

As a visionary founder, your first team members will shape everything. Choose wisely. Here are the roles you should prioritize:

Role	Description
Integrator	Turns your big ideas into clear steps. Handles execution and systems.
Creative Architect	Handles branding, design, and communication of the vision.
Tech Lead / Developer	If you're building a tech-based idea, you need someone who understands and executes.
Operations Lead	Ensures smooth backend operations—logistics, vendors, suppliers.
Customer Advocate	Focused on understanding and obsessing over your target users.

Start lean. Choose high-impact, flexible thinkers who can wear multiple hats.

From My Experience: JAY T CLOTHING & Justech International

When I built JAY T CLOTHING and Justech International, I realized early that **I wasn't looking for staff—I was looking for soldiers of possibility.**

The real growth began when I stopped hiring only for skills and started building a **culture of belief**. I mentored each team member, aligned them with the vision, and created platforms where their creativity could thrive.

The result? A team that doesn't just build for the brand — they build with me.

Common Mistakes Visionaries Make

- **Hiring based on friendship, not fit**
- **Avoiding confrontation instead of developing people**
- **Delegating too soon without clear expectations**
- **Failing to document core values and culture early**

Avoid these errors. You're not just hiring — you're **architecting a future.**

Quote to Remember

"You can build a business with employees. But if you want to build a revolution, you need believers."
— Justine Ehiwario, The Architect of Possibilities

Action Exercise

1. Write down your 3 core values as a leader.
2. List the 5 most essential qualities you want in your core team.

3. Identify one area where you need to upgrade your team this year.

Final Thought: Alone You Build, Together You Dominate

Building with giants means choosing **alignment over convenience**, **values over credentials**, and **purpose over payroll**.

Possibility Teams are not just a tool for success—they are the **very engine** of transformation.

Chapter 4:

The Blueprint Principle – Turning Ideas Into Scalable Systems

"Great empires are not built on energy alone — they are built on engineered efficiency."
— Justine Ehiwario

Why Every Vision Needs a Blueprint

A visionary idea without structure is like a skyscraper without a foundation. You may have the most disruptive, revolutionary idea in the world — but if it can't be replicated, automated, scaled, or sustained, then it will collapse under its own ambition.

In *The Unstoppable Road to Wealth Creation*, I emphasized:

"Your vision must be strong enough to inspire and structured enough to multiply."

That's the essence of the **Blueprint Principle**. It's about turning genius into **a system** — something that can run, grow, and evolve without burning out the founder.

What Is a Blueprint?

A **Blueprint** is a replicable, step-by-step framework that allows your business or idea to:

- Operate without micromanagement
- Deliver consistent quality and results
- Grow sustainably
- Attract investors, partners, and collaborators

It is the **architecture of execution** — the invisible structure behind visible success.

The Blueprint Process: From Vision to System

There are five powerful stages in building a blueprint that can scale:

1. Ideation: Clarify the Core Value Proposition

At this stage, ask:

- What problem are you solving?
- Who is it for?
- What transformation do you offer?

Your idea should be:

- **Clear** – easily explainable in one sentence
- **Compelling** – it moves people emotionally or intellectually

- **Credible** – backed by real insights, data, or experience

Example:

Airbnb started with the idea: "What if people could rent out a room to strangers for a night?"

Clear. Compelling. Credible. That was the seed of a $100B company.

2. Modeling: Design the Framework of Delivery

This is the "how" stage.

- How will the idea be delivered consistently?
- What is the customer journey?
- What are the core activities, tools, people, and technologies involved?

Map out the **workflow**: from the first customer interaction to the final product delivery.

You're building the skeleton here — the **engine of execution**.

3. Systemization: Create Repeatable Processes

Now turn each part of your model into a **system**.

A system is:

- Documented
- Teachable
- Repeatable

- Measurable

Systems bring **predictability** and **stability**.

"If your business depends entirely on your presence, you don't have a business — you have a job."
— *Justine Ehiwario, The DNA of Financial Greatness*

4. Automation: Leverage Tools and Technology

The next level is automation. Use tools to handle what doesn't require human creativity:

- CRMs
- Email sequences
- Sales funnels
- Scheduling tools
- Inventory and order systems
- AI assistants

Your goal is to **free up human creativity** by letting machines handle the routine.

5. Optimization: Measure, Refine, Improve

No system is perfect. Build **feedback loops** to track:

- What's working?
- What's slowing you down?

- Where are customers dropping off?
- Which part of the process needs innovation?

Optimization turns a good system into a **world-class operation**.

The Visionary Trap: Micromanagement

Many entrepreneurs fail here.

They want control so much that they refuse to build systems. But control without systems leads to **burnout, bottlenecks, and breakdowns**.

You can't scale greatness if only **you** can deliver it. You must **engineer yourself out of the day-to-day**.

From My Playbook: Scaling JAY T CLOTHING

At first, I did everything — designs, customer service, printing, delivery. But I quickly realized: **growth was not possible without systems.**

So I created:

- A design process blueprint
- A customer ordering and feedback system
- A social media automation schedule
- A production and fulfilment framework

Each of these allowed us to scale, multiply output, and deliver **consistent excellence** — even when I wasn't physically present.

Key Areas Where You Must Build Blueprints

Area	Blueprint Focus
Customer Experience	Journey from discovery to loyalty
Marketing	How you attract, nurture, and convert leads
Operations	Daily activities that keep the business running
Finance	Cash flow, expenses, invoicing, pricing strategy
Hiring	Onboarding, training, team development
Product/Service Delivery	Step-by-step structure for fulfillment

Tools for System Builders

Here are some tools you can use to design and implement blueprints:

- **Trello / Notion / Asana** – Project & process management
- **Zapier / Make** – Automation between platforms
- **Loom / SOP Videos** – Training and onboarding tools
- **Google Docs / Templates** – Documentation and playbooks
- **CRM systems** – Managing client relationships

Blueprint Mindset Shift

Most people think:

"Let me figure it out and hustle through it."

Visionaries think:

"Let me build it once so it works without me 100 times."

Systems build wealth that **lasts beyond the founder.**
Blueprints build empires that **outlive the visionary.**

Quote to Remember

"The most valuable part of your business is not your product — it's your process."
— Justine Ehiwario

Action Tasks

1. Identify one chaotic or manual area in your business.
2. Write down the current process, step by step.
3. Document and simplify that process.
4. Test it with someone else to see if it's repeatable.
5. Explore tools that could automate at least one step.

Final Insight: Structure is the Silent Force of Scale

Great businesses are not built on talent alone. They are built on frameworks, principles, and engineered consistency.

If your vision is the **dream**, then your blueprint is the **bridge.**

Justine Ehiwario

Chapter 5:

The Power of Iteration – Mastering the Art of Evolving Your Idea Without Losing Its Core

"Innovation is not a one-time stroke of genius. It's the courage to keep editing your masterpiece."
— Justine Ehiwario

Iteration Is the Lifeline of Greatness

Many people imagine success as a straight line from idea to impact. But in truth, greatness emerges through **iteration** — the consistent improvement, refinement, and reimagining of your product, service, or idea while preserving its foundational essence.

In *The Mind of a Trillionaire*, I wrote:

"Don't fall in love with the version of your idea. Fall in love with the impact it's meant to create."

Iteration is what turns good ideas into legendary movements. Every visionary enterprise — from Apple to Amazon — went through cycles of refining their model before global adoption.

The Core vs. The Container

Think of your idea like water and the cup it's poured into:

- The **core** of your idea is its essence — the problem you solve, the value you deliver, the mission you pursue.
- The **container** is the method, platform, brand, or delivery system.

Iteration often involves **changing the container** without diluting the **core**.

Example:

- Netflix began as a DVD rental service. That was the container.
- Its core? Entertainment on demand. That hasn't changed — just the medium has.

Great entrepreneurs protect the **purpose**, but are bold enough to **change the presentation**.

Iteration in Action: 4 Key Areas to Focus On

1. Product Iteration

Your first version is rarely your best. Market feedback reveals what real people want — not what you assume they want.

"If you're not embarrassed by the first version of your product, you launched too late."
— Reid Hoffman, LinkedIn Co-Founder

How to iterate:

- Launch a Minimum Viable Product (MVP)
- Collect user feedback early and often
- Improve features based on real behaviour

2. Process Iteration

Are your systems delivering results efficiently and consistently?

"Every system must evolve or it will eventually collapse under its own weight."
— Justine Ehiwario, The DNA of Financial Greatness

How to iterate:

- Track KPIs across departments
- Identify bottlenecks
- Improve turnaround time and reduce redundancy

3. Customer Experience Iteration

What do people feel when they interact with your brand?

"The emotional resonance of your brand is more valuable than the functionality of your product."

How to iterate:

- Improve customer support
- Enhance onboarding experience
- Personalize engagement

Scenario:

At JAY T CLOTHING, we added a custom design assistant after repeated feedback about indecision in design choices. That one tweak led to a 35% increase in completed orders.

4. Brand & Market Positioning Iteration

Markets change. Your relevance depends on your ability to adapt.

How to iterate:

- Refresh your visual identity or messaging
- Explore new customer segments
- Pivot without compromising purpose

Iteration ≠ Insecurity

Some fear that changing their product or strategy is a sign of inconsistency.

But true inconsistency is:

- Refusing to change while results deteriorate.
- Ignoring feedback in favour of ego.

- Being loyal to your method, not your mission.

"Iteration is not doubt — it is devotion to excellence."

Case Study: Amazon's Relentless Evolution

Amazon started as an online bookstore. But Jeff Bezos knew the real mission: **to become the most customer-centric company on earth.**

From books, it evolved to:

- Multi-product e-commerce
- Amazon Prime
- Cloud computing (AWS)
- Alexa and smart devices
- Physical stores

Same core. New iterations.

Today, AWS powers much of the internet — a far leap from its original bookstore identity.

A Simple Framework for Effective Iteration (The 5-I Model)

Step	Description
1. Identify	Pinpoint what needs improvement.
2. Investigate	Collect feedback, analyze data, and study the market.
3. Ideate	Brainstorm possible enhancements.
4. Implement	Apply your changes with a controlled rollout.
5. Iterate Again	Test, refine, and evolve further.

Tools and Habits for Iterative Entrepreneurs

- **Surveys & Forms:** Google Forms, Typeform
- **User Testing:** Beta testing groups
- **Data Analysis:** Google Analytics, Mixpanel, Hotjar
- **A/B Testing:** Try two versions to see which performs better
- **Feedback Loops:** Weekly team retrospectives or customer reviews.

Iteration Quotes for Visionaries

"Progress is impossible without change, and those who cannot change their minds cannot change anything."
— George Bernard Shaw

"Your brand is a living entity. It breathes. It evolves. Let it."
— Justine Ehiwario

Action Tasks for Entrepreneurs

1. Identify one feature of your product or service that hasn't evolved in 12 months.
2. Collect feedback from 10 users or customers.
3. Map out at least 3 potential improvements.
4. Implement one change this week and track the result.
5. Schedule a monthly "Iteration Day" in your team.

Final Insight: You Don't Need to Be Right the First Time

The world doesn't reward **perfectionists** — it rewards **refiners**.

Legendary businesses are not born fully formed. They are shaped by trial, refinement, listening, and adaptation.

"You are not building a monument — you are shaping a movement. Keep sculpting."

Justine Ehiwario

Chapter 6:

Strategic Partnerships – The Hidden Leverage Behind Big Impact

"If you want to go fast, go alone. If you want to go far, go together."
— African Proverb

"The wealth of tomorrow is hidden in the strength of your relationships today."
— Justine Ehiwario, The Things Wealthy People Do

The Era of Collaboration Over Competition

In the age of hyper-connectivity, solo genius is no longer enough. The world's most disruptive enterprises — from Tesla to TikTok — are built not just on ideas, but on **strategic alliances** that accelerated growth, expanded reach, and amplified value.

Strategic partnerships are **deliberate alliances** formed to:

- Leverage each other's strengths
- Share resources
- Enter new markets
- Co-create innovative solutions

"The most scalable ideas in history were never scaled alone."

What Makes a Partnership Strategic?

Not every collaboration is a strategic partnership. A **strategic partnership** is defined by three characteristics:

1. **Mutual Benefit**

   Both parties gain value — financially, operationally, or in terms of reach.

2. **Shared Vision**

   Alignment in long-term purpose and strategic direction.

3. **Complementary Strengths**

   Each partner brings something unique and vital to the table.

Case Studies of Game-Changing Strategic Partnerships

1. Apple & Nike (Nike+)

Apple brought its ecosystem, Nike brought athletic performance. Together, they created the Nike+ wearable fitness tracker — a product that revolutionized sports tech.

2. Starbucks & Spotify

Baristas got Spotify Premium, and customers could influence in-store playlists. Starbucks increased digital engagement; Spotify gained users and visibility.

3. Jay T Solutions & Justech International

In our own ecosystem, Jay T Solutions provides branding power, while Justech International powers tech implementation. This synergy has led to the seamless delivery of high-tech, branded solutions to a wide range of clients — maximizing both impact and client satisfaction.

Why Visionaries Rely on Partnerships

Let's break down the leverage you gain:

Type of Leverage	What It Offers	Example
Financial Leverage	Shared investment, reduced risk	Co-funding R&D with a tech firm
Market Leverage	Access to new demographics and geographies	Partnering with a local distributor
Credibility Leverage	Trust borrowed from established brands	Endorsement by a respected industry leader
Innovation Leverage	Co-developing products or systems	A joint venture in AI tech

"You don't need to own everything — you just need access to it."

Personal Insight: How Partnerships Grew My Vision

In the publishing of *The Mind of a Trillionaire*, I collaborated with editors, proof-readers, graphic designers, and distribution platforms. Each played a part in making the book a reality.

Types of Strategic Partnerships You Can Build

Type	Best For	Example
Equity Partnerships	Long-term joint ventures	Tech firm co-building an app
Marketing Partnerships	Increasing visibility & leads	Influencer campaigns or co-branded content
Operational Partnerships	Reducing cost & boosting output	Shared warehousing or fulfillment
Technology Partnerships	Enhancing digital presence	APIs, software integration
Distribution Partnerships	Reaching new customers	Selling through another company's platform
Licensing Partnerships	Monetizing IP or branding	Clothing with licensed cartoon characters

Key Principles to Build Powerful Partnerships

1. Know Your Value

What do you bring to the table? Skills? Audience? Infrastructure? Never enter a partnership from a place of weakness or desperation.

2. Align Values

Vision misalignment is the #1 cause of partnership failure. Ensure you're building in the same direction.

3. Start Small, Scale Later

Test the waters with a pilot project before diving in with equity or capital.

4. Define Clear Terms

Spell out responsibilities, expectations, IP rights, revenue splits, and exit clauses.

5. Invest in the Relationship

People do business with people. Don't just communicate—connect. Create time for appreciation, brainstorming, and conflict resolution.

Common Mistakes in Strategic Partnerships

1. **Chasing Big Names Without Strategy**
   Just because someone is famous or successful doesn't mean they're the right partner.

2. **Overpromising, Under-Delivering**

   Don't exaggerate what you bring. Be honest and reliable.

3. **Failing to Put it in Writing**

   Always formalize agreements. Verbal promises are
   dangerous in business.

4. **Ignoring Culture Fit**

   Different working styles and values can break a partnership
   faster than numbers.

Partnership Preparation Toolkit

Before entering a strategic partnership, ask:

- What specific value do I bring?
- What do I need from the partner?
- How does this support my long-term mission?
- What's the minimum viable collaboration we can test?
- What's the worst-case scenario, and how do I mitigate it?

"Strategic partnerships don't just add — they multiply."

Action Tasks for the Architect of Possibilities

1. Identify 3 brands or businesses in your industry that
   complement what you offer.

2. Research them and list areas where you can bring value.

3. Reach out with a co-creation or value-sharing idea.

4. Pilot a small initiative together and evaluate results.

5. Document the experience, learn, and iterate.

Quotes to Remember

"Greatness doesn't grow in isolation — it expands through collaboration."
— Justine Ehiwario

"A single relationship can open doors that strategy alone cannot."

"The right partnership can make ten years' work happen in one."

Final Insight: Your Network is Your Net Worth

A true visionary understands that possibilities are not just built with bricks of innovation — they are scaled with bridges of partnership.

Don't just build your dream — connect it to others. In the connections lie your next elevation.

Chapter 7:

From Vision to Execution – Turning Concepts into Concrete Business Models

"Ideas are easy. Execution is everything."
— John Doerr, Venture Capitalist

"A dream without a blueprint is just a fantasy."
— Justine Ehiwario, The Unstoppable Road to Wealth Creation

The Execution Gap: Where Many Dreams Die

Every successful entrepreneur begins with a compelling idea. But here's the reality: **the world doesn't reward good ideas—it rewards executed ideas.**

Thousands of people may share your vision, but what sets apart the few who build game-changing businesses is **their ability to translate concepts into operational business models.**

A visionary becomes an architect of possibilities when they master this bridge from **inspiration to implementation.**

The Architecture of Execution

Think of your business model as the **blueprint** that connects your vision with the real world.

To build it, you need:

Element	Purpose	Key Questions
Value Proposition	Defines your unique solution	What problem are you solving? Why does it matter?
Target Audience	Identifies your ideal customer	Who needs this solution and why?
Revenue Model	Determines how you make money	How do you generate income?
Cost Structure	Understands your expenses	What will it cost to build and operate?
Delivery Channels	Outlines how you reach your market	How will you deliver your product or service?
Key Resources & Activities	Lists what you need and must do	What assets and actions are essential to success?
Strategic Partners	Highlights collaborative leverage	Who can help you move faster and smarter?

"Execution is the canvas where the masterpiece of vision is painted."

Building the Right Business Model

You don't need a perfect model; you need a **workable and testable** one. Start with the **Lean Canvas** approach:

1. **Identify the problem** your customer faces.
2. **Define your solution**—clearly and simply.
3. **Test early** with minimal investment (Minimum Viable Product).
4. **Gather feedback** and iterate quickly.
5. **Measure traction**—not vanity metrics, but revenue, retention, and referrals.

Example: Jay T Clothing

What began as a clothing idea was executed into a business model by:

- Identifying a gap in customized urban fashion.
- Building a print-on-demand model that eliminated upfront inventory.
- Leveraging partnerships with platforms like Shopify, Amazon, and Printify.
- Tapping into youth and event markets globally.

The result? A brand that operates lean, scales fast, and adapts to changing trends.

Tools for Execution

Use these tools to move from idea to impact:

Tool	Purpose
Business Model Canvas	Visual framework for planning
Trello / Notion / Asana	Organize and track progress
Figma / Canva	Prototype your product design
Google Workspace / Slack	Collaborate efficiently
QuickBooks / Xero	Manage finances and budgets
Stripe / PayPal / Flutterwave	Handle online payments

Real-Life Insight: Vision Means Nothing Without Movement

When I launched **Jay T Prime Properties**, the initial idea was big—but I had to start small. We didn't build mansions on day one. We started with affordable renovations and built a portfolio. Today, the same vision now serves premium and luxury clients.

I followed a rule I call the **"Minimum Realization Principle"**:

What's the smallest real version of this idea I can launch to the market?

This forces clarity and drives immediate action.

Vision Iteration: Your Model Will Evolve

The business model you start with will not be the one you scale with. Netflix started as a DVD delivery service. Amazon sold only books. Tesla began with one luxury sports car.

Execution requires:

- **Adaptability**
- **Relentless feedback**
- **Patience in growth, urgency in learning**

"The idea that wins is not always the first idea—it's the one that evolves."

From Blueprint to Building: Execution Steps

1. **Sketch your business model** on one page.
2. **Validate your value proposition** through real conversations with potential users.
3. **Launch a simple version** of your product or service.
4. **Track what works**—and drop what doesn't.
5. **Use momentum wisely** to reinvest and refine your offering.

Common Mistakes in Execution

1. **Overthinking instead of testing**

   Perfect plans on paper are no match for real-world tests.

2. **Waiting for the "right time"**

   There is never a perfect time. Start where you are.

3. **Building in isolation**

   Without feedback, you'll end up solving the wrong problem.

4. **Chasing funding before product-market fit**

   Investors don't fund ideas—they fund traction.

The DNA of Execution-Driven Entrepreneurs

"Ideas excite, but execution empowers."

— Justine Ehiwario

Execution architects share a mindset that includes:

- **Discipline over distraction**

- **Clarity over complexity**

- **Action over assumption**

- **Learning over ego**

Action Steps for Today's Visionary

- Write your idea in one sentence.

- Use the Business Model Canvas to map out the model.

- Create a Minimum Viable Product in 7 days.

- Show it to 10 people and gather their honest feedback.

- Refine, relaunch, and repeat until it sticks.

Quotes to Remember

"The vision is the compass. The business model is the engine. Execution is the fuel."

"Don't just start a business. Build a model that can live, breathe, and grow."

"The world needs more finishers than dreamers."

Justine Ehiwario

Chapter 8:

Mastering Risk and Embracing Failure – How Setbacks Can Sharpen Your Success

"Success is not built on success. It's built on failure. It's built on frustration. Sometimes it's built on catastrophe."
— Sumner Redstone

"Failure is not the opposite of success; it is part of the process."
— *Justine Ehiwario, The Mind of a Trillionaire*

The Myth of the Smooth Journey

Ask anyone who has built a legendary business, and they'll tell you: **there is no straight line to success**. Entrepreneurs who change the world are not those who avoid risk or failure—they are the ones who face it head-on, learn fast, and rise stronger.

Yet, in a world addicted to polished highlight reels, we often forget that behind every win lies a **trail of stumbles, scars, and second chances**.

"There is no glory without grit."

Risk: The Currency of Innovation

If you're building something truly ground-breaking, **you will face risk**:

- Financial risk
- Market risk
- Reputational risk
- Operational risk
- Emotional and psychological risk

But risk is not the enemy—it's the **toll gate to breakthrough**.

In *The DNA of Financial Greatness*, I described risk as a **creative tension**—the necessary friction that polishes diamonds and perfects ideas. Great innovators do not gamble blindly; they **calculate, mitigate, and move forward despite uncertainty.**

"Risk doesn't mean recklessness. It means readiness to walk into the unknown with a plan and purpose."
— Justine Ehiwario

The Role of Failure in Breakthroughs

Let's be clear—**you will fail.**

The real question is: **how will you respond when you do?**

Failure is a teacher—ruthless, but effective. It:

- Reveals blind spots
- Builds resilience
- Sharpens focus
- Refines the mission
- Exposes who you are and what you're made of

"Some of my best strategies were born out of my worst failures."

Reframing Failure: Not a Dead End, But a Detour

Here's how to **reframe and recover from failure**:

Old View	New Mindset
I failed.	I discovered what doesn't work.
I lost everything.	I learned what's truly valuable.
I'm not good enough.	I'm becoming better.
This was a waste.	This was tuition in the school of mastery.

"Failure is feedback—not finality."

Case Studies of Visionaries Who Failed Forward

1. Elon Musk

Tesla and SpaceX both flirted with bankruptcy multiple times. Musk took personal financial risks that left him nearly broke. But those lessons birthed a tighter business model, better innovation practices, and ultimately, two industry-shaking giants.

2. Walt Disney

He was fired from a newspaper job for "lack of imagination" and had multiple failed ventures. Yet he learned, pivoted, and built an empire of imagination.

3. You

Your own setbacks—whether personal, financial, or professional—are not wasted. Every failure has brought you closer to clarity. You're still standing. You're still building. That's winning.

How to Build a Healthy Relationship with Risk and Failure

1. **Expect it**

   The journey will include roadblocks. Don't be surprised. Be prepared.

2. **Study it**

   Deconstruct every setback like a case study. Find the root. Extract the lesson.

3. **Insure against it**

   Put structures in place: savings buffers, legal protections, advisory boards.

4. **Talk about it**

   Vulnerability is strength. Share your lessons with others. It builds trust and community.

5. **Bounce, don't break**

   Cultivate resilience. Mentally rehearse recovery—not just success.

Practical Framework: The R.I.S.K Model

Here's a simple decision tool for dealing with risk:

R – Recognize	Understand the nature of the risk you're facing.
I – Investigate	Gather data, weigh outcomes, and assess impact.
S – Strategize	Develop a response plan—accept, avoid, reduce, or transfer.
K – Keep Moving	Don't stall forever. Action, even imperfect, creates clarity.

Turning Setbacks into Superpowers

"The obstacle is not in the way. It is the way."
— Marcus Aurelius

Here's how to transmute failures into fuel:

- **Build a "Lessons Log"**: Every failure gets documented, debriefed, and translated into future wisdom.

- **Celebrate Post-Mortems**: Analyse what went wrong without shame—treat it like a business scientist.

- **Mentor Through Mistakes**: Share your story with upcoming visionaries. Your scars can be someone's strategy.

Mindset Shifts of the Architect of Possibilities

- From **perfectionism** to **progress**.
- From **fear** to **feedback**.
- From **avoidance** to **awareness**.
- From **failure-resistant** to **failure-resilient**.

The Possibility in Pain

Your journey will have setbacks. But every vision that changes the world has one thing in common: it survived the valley and kept moving.

Don't run from risk. Don't fear failure. Master both—and you'll shape industries, transform lives, and leave a lasting legacy.

"Your scars are not signs of shame; they're symbols of survival."
— *Justine Ehiwario, The Things Wealthy People Do*

Justine Ehiwario

Chapter 9:

Building the Dream Team – Attracting, Aligning, and Empowering Talented People Who Share Your Vision

"Great things in business are never done by one person. They're done by a team of people."
— Steve Jobs

"Behind every monumental business is not only a visionary—but a visionary with a tribe of believers."
— Justine Ehiwario, The Mind of a Trillionaire

Introduction: The Power of People

No matter how ground-breaking your idea, how brilliant your strategy, or how bold your ambition—if you don't surround yourself with the right people, your dream will remain a sketch on paper. In the journey of building an industry-shaping business, your greatest leverage is not capital or code—it's human talent aligned with your purpose.

A visionary doesn't just build a company; they architect a culture and attract the right minds to co-create a movement.

In this chapter, we explore how to attract, align, and empower a dream team that helps you not only achieve your goals—but exceed them.

1. Vision First, People Next

The foundation of any dream team is a compelling vision. Talented people don't just work for money—they work for meaning. Visionary entrepreneurs attract the best not because of what they offer, but because of what they stand for.

The question every potential team member silently asks is: "Why should I build this with you?"

Takeaway: Before hiring, mentoring, or delegating—clarify your "why" and live it audibly.

2. Hire for Culture, Train for Skill

Visionaries don't just hire resumes—they recruit culture carriers.

Yes, technical competence is important, but **culture fit is non-negotiable**. Why? Because skills can be taught, but values, mindset, and attitude are deep-rooted.

Ask yourself:

- Does this person align with our values?
- Do they thrive in our pace and style?
- Do they take ownership and show initiative?

Tip: Build hiring scorecards with cultural alignment as a key metric.

3. The Three Types of Team Members Every Visionary Needs

Every business needs a blend of personalities and strengths. The visionary's job is to assemble a complementary mix. Think of it like building a superhero squad.

The Architect: Thinkers and planners who love designing systems, structures, and scalable processes. They ground the visionary's ideas into reality.

The Builder: Doers, executors, and problem-solvers who thrive on momentum. They move fast, adapt quickly, and value performance.

The Guardian: Culture custodians, mentors, and morale boosters. They protect the spirit of the team and ensure values aren't compromised.

Build with this triad in mind. You don't need carbon copies—you need collaborators with different superpowers.

4. Empowerment Over Micromanagement

Visionaries don't build greatness by holding the reins too tightly. You attract top performers by creating environments where they can lead, innovate, and take ownership.

Empower your team by:

- Sharing the big picture often
- Giving autonomy with accountability
- Encouraging failure-based learning
- Recognizing initiative, not just results

In my book The Things Wealthy People Do, I described empowerment as the entrepreneurial equivalent of compounding interest. The more you invest trust in your team, the more returns you reap in creativity, loyalty, and momentum.

At Jay T Prime Properties, our top-performing agents are not those who follow scripts but those who feel empowered to bring new strategies, pitch bold ideas, and even make executive decisions within reason.

5. **Alignment: The Invisible Glue**

Your dream team is only as effective as its alignment.

Alignment happens when:

- Everyone understands the mission
- Individual goals match organizational goals
- Roles are clearly defined
- Feedback is frequent and transparent
- Success is celebrated collectively

Misalignment is subtle but dangerous. It shows up as duplicated effort, friction in decision-making, and unspoken dissatisfaction. As the architect, your job is to constantly adjust the gears to keep the machine running smoothly.

Monthly vision syncs, transparent KPIs, and performance retrospectives are crucial tools we use across all Jay T companies to ensure we're rowing in the same direction.

6. Case Study: Building the JAY T CLOTHING Team

When I launched JAY T CLOTHING, I didn't just need designers—I needed dreamers. People who could see beyond the stitches and screen prints. I hired based on fire, not finesse.

One of our early employees had zero formal fashion experience—but she had an eye for culture, a love for design, and an obsession with storytelling. Today, she leads our limited-edition creative campaigns globally.

Our greatest wins have come from people who believed in the mission even when the systems were still messy. They co-created our brand identity and built processes with me, not just for me.

That's what makes a dream team—they help shape the dream.

7. The Visionary as Chief People Officer

As a founder, your most important role is not strategy—it's stewardship of people.

Your calendar should reflect this:

- Weekly 1:1s
- Leadership coaching
- Culture reinforcement
- Hiring and talent development
- Conflict resolution

Even if you outsource HR, never outsource heart. You must remain visible, accessible, and intentional about cultivating the environment your team thrives in.

Remember: You don't just hire hands—you invite hearts.

8. Red Flags to Watch Out For

Not everyone belongs on your dream team. Watch for:

- Chronic blame or excuse-making
- Resistance to feedback or change
- Low emotional intelligence
- Ego that overshadows the mission
- Misalignment of personal and team goals

Sometimes, subtraction is growth. Don't hesitate to prune to protect the vision.

9. Investing in Your Team

The best leaders don't just extract value from their team—they pour into them.

Invest through:

- Training and professional development
- Mental health support
- Flexible work policies
- Equity, bonuses, and profit-sharing
- Recognition and promotion opportunities

People stay where they feel seen, valued, and challenged.

As I wrote in The Unstoppable Road to Wealth Creation: "People build the wealth—and the right people preserve it."

10. Summary: Your Dream Team Is Your Legacy

The businesses that change the world are built by teams that believe in a shared mission, execute with autonomy, and grow with unity. Visionaries don't just attract talent—they cultivate it, empower it, and walk with it.

Your team will outlast your ideas. Build with that in mind.

Final Quote:

"A visionary sees the future. A team brings it into the present." — Justine Ehiwario

Chapter 10:

Crafting a Culture of Innovation — How to Make Creativity a Core Operating System

"Innovation distinguishes between a leader and a follower."
— Steve Jobs

"Creativity is not a department. It's the atmosphere in which game-changing businesses breathe."
— Justine Ehiwario, The Mind of a Trillionaire

Introduction: Innovation as a Daily Habit, Not an Annual Event

Too often, businesses treat innovation as a one-time project or an annual brainstorming retreat. But real innovation—the kind that redefines industries and solves complex global problems—is not sporadic. It's systematic. It's embedded into the DNA of an organization.

In this chapter, we'll explore how visionary entrepreneurs turn innovation into an operating system. We'll look at how to foster creative thinking, design systems that support experimentation, and build a company culture where innovation flows organically.

1. **The Myth of the Lone Genius**

   Contrary to popular belief, innovation doesn't come from a lone genius having a lightbulb moment in isolation. In reality, breakthrough ideas often emerge from teams that operate in high-trust environments with the freedom to explore, test, and fail.

Takeaway: Innovation is not genius-driven; it's culture-enabled.

2. **Create a Safe Space for Failure**

   You cannot have a culture of innovation without building a culture of psychological safety. Innovation means risk. Risk implies failure. If people are afraid of being punished for getting it wrong, they'll never try anything new.

Tip: Publicly celebrate lessons learned from failed experiments. Make risk-taking part of your reward system.

3. **Make Curiosity a Core Value**

   Innovation starts with curiosity—the relentless desire to ask, "What if?" and "Why not?"

One of the first lessons I teach at any Jay T company onboarding is this: "You were not hired to follow instructions. You were hired to question, improve, and reimagine."

Encourage your team to:

- Ask better questions

- Explore emerging technologies
- Read across disciplines
- Attend conferences outside your core field

Curiosity creates the conditions for serendipity—those unexpected sparks that ignite innovation.

4. **Build an Idea Pipeline**

   An innovative culture requires an engine that captures, vets, and develops ideas consistently—not just during annual planning.

Here's how to build an internal innovation pipeline:

- Idea Capture Tools: Use shared digital whiteboards, innovation portals, or Slack channels for submissions.
- Triage Sessions: Regularly review ideas based on potential impact and feasibility.
- Prototype Labs: Allocate resources to rapidly prototype and test promising concepts.
- Feedback Loops: Involve real customers early in the ideation phase.

At JAY T CLOTHING, our custom glow-in-the-dark print line was born from a junior staffer's casual suggestion logged in our idea tracker. Within three months, it became a top-selling product for festival season.

Lesson: Everyone should feel they have permission to contribute creatively.

5. **Democratize Innovation**

    Innovation isn't reserved for R&D or product teams—it should be everybody's job.

Innovation happens when:

- The frontline is empowered to solve problems
- Incentives are aligned with experimentation
- Communication flows vertically and horizontally

Action Step: Create cross-functional innovation squads to tackle real problems.

6. **Protect Deep Work & Thinking Time**

    Creative ideas rarely emerge in back-to-back meetings. You need uninterrupted time for reflection and synthesis.

Encourage your team to block out thinking time. Consider instituting:

- No-meeting afternoons
- Weekly "Innovation Hours"
- Creative retreats or digital sabbaticals

Creativity isn't a side hustle. It's the foundation of reinvention.

7. **Lead by Example: Be the Chief Innovator**

   As a visionary, your actions shape what your team prioritizes. If you want an innovative culture, you must model curiosity, risk-taking, and a hunger for what's next.

I make it a practice to:

- Share articles on trends and emerging tech weekly
- Ask challenging "what if" questions during reviews
- Invite open dissent and debate during strategic planning
- Publicly recognize those who break the mould.

Leadership that stifles experimentation unintentionally poisons innovation. Your team needs to see you imagining, iterating, and occasionally failing.

8. **Institutionalize Continuous Learning**

   An innovative company is a learning company. Build infrastructure for skill-building and mental expansion.

Ideas:

- Company-wide book clubs on disruptive thinking
- Sponsored online courses and conferences
- Internal TED-style talks
- Innovation mentors and guilds

In The Things Wealthy People Do, I wrote that "your learning velocity determines your earning velocity." The same applies to organizations—what you don't know will eventually cost you.

Make learning part of your employee experience, not just a benefit.

9. **Innovation Metrics: What Gets Measured Gets Reinforced**

   To make innovation sustainable, track it. Consider measuring:

   - Number of new ideas submitted per employee
   - Time from idea to prototype
   - Percentage of revenue from new products/services
   - ROI from experimental projects
   - Employee engagement around innovation programs

Don't let innovation become a buzzword. Make it a benchmark.

10. **The Innovation Flywheel: How It All Comes Together**

    Once embedded, your culture of innovation becomes a self-perpetuating flywheel:

    Curiosity → Ideas → Prototypes → Feedback → Iteration → Success → Motivation → More Curiosity

Each cycle strengthens the next. Over time, innovation becomes your identity—not just your initiative.

Final Thought:

"Innovation is not about adding something new—it's about seeing with new eyes."

— Justine Ehiwario

As the architect of possibility, your greatest asset is not the blueprint in your hand, but the culture you craft. A culture where creativity is oxygen, and innovation is the native language.

Chapter 11:

The Scalability Blueprint: Systems, Automation, and Replication without Losing Soul

"There is no greatness where there is no system."

– Will Durant

"Scale is not just growth in size—it is growth in impact, in reach, and in operational harmony. But if you scale chaos, you get bigger chaos. Scale excellence, and you multiply impact."

– Justine Ehiwario, The Unstoppable Road to Wealth Creation

Introduction: Why Scale Is Not Optional.

If you've built something valuable—a product, service, or system that solves a real problem—then you owe it to the world to make it accessible at scale. Scaling is not about ego. It's about stewardship. It's about giving your ideas legs so they can run farther than you ever could alone.

But here's the paradox: many great businesses collapse during scale because they fail to systematize operations, automate effectively, or replicate their culture. Worse yet, some scale so rigidly that they lose their soul—the personal touch, the agility, the "why" behind their brand.

This chapter is your blueprint for achieving scale with both precision and humanity.

1. **Understand What You're Scaling (And Why)**
   Before you attempt to scale anything, get brutally clear on what is truly worth scaling.

Ask yourself:

- What part of your business delivers the most value?
- What is most profitable or impactful?
- What part of your process is teachable, repeatable, and documentable?
- What still requires your genius, and what doesn't?

For instance, when we expanded JAY T CLOTHING's customized T-shirt line globally, we didn't try to scale every style. We focused on the most in-demand categories (family designs, kids' birthday outfits, and glow-in-the-dark prints) and built fulfilment pipelines around them.

Scale starts with focus.

2. **Build Repeatable Systems**
   As I wrote in The Things Wealthy People Do, "Systems liberate visionaries." Without repeatable systems, your

business is like a machine that requires constant manual cranking. Systems allow you to replicate your excellence without replicating your effort.

Elements of scalable systems:

- Standard Operating Procedures (SOPs)
- Workflow automation tools
- CRM and task management platforms
- Documented onboarding and training programs
- Visual dashboards for performance tracking

Tip: Systemize what works so others can reproduce it without diluting quality.

3. **Automate the Mundane, Not the Magical**

   Automation is the muscle of scalability—but it must be applied with discernment. Automate repetitive tasks, but never automate the parts of your business that require creativity, empathy, or deep human judgment.

Use automation for:

- Email campaigns and client follow-ups
- Inventory updates and invoicing
- Social media scheduling
- Customer support ticket routing
- Lead scoring and CRM updates

Avoid automating:

- Creative consultations
- High-touch sales interactions
- Personalized customer service
- Internal culture-building rituals

Balance scale with soul.

4. **Build for Replication, Not Just Growth**

   Growth is linear. Replication is exponential.

Design your business in a way that it can be cloned, franchised, or expanded across regions without requiring you to be everywhere.

Replication means:

- You train others to do what you do
- You license or franchise your business model
- You partner with local operators under your brand
- You create plug-and-play toolkits others can use

Key Point: Replication requires codifying your culture, not just your workflows.

5. **Empower Without Abdicating**

   Delegation is not abdication. As your business scales, you must learn to empower others while maintaining oversight. This is the essence of operational maturity.

Create structures for:

- Tiered decision-making authority
- KPIs and accountability metrics
- Leadership development and mentorship
- Clear escalation protocols

As I emphasized in The Architect of Possibilities, "You must grow people as you grow processes."

6. **Preserve Culture Intentionally**

   Culture doesn't scale automatically—it must be engineered.

The danger: as your team grows, your founding principles can become diluted, misinterpreted, or forgotten. That's why visionary founders must embed culture in every system and touchpoint.

Ways to scale culture:

- Document your core values and origin story
- Hire for mindset, not just skillset
- Use storytelling during onboarding and all-hands meetings
- Celebrate small wins that reinforce your mission
- Create internal rituals that express your brand identity

At all Jay T companies, we reinforce the mindset of excellence, ownership, and creativity in weekly briefings, internal awards, and daily language.

Culture is the soul of your business—tend it with care.

7. **Protect Quality at Scale**

   One of the greatest threats to scalability is declining quality.
   You can't compromise your standard just to meet demand.

Use the following tools:

- Quality assurance teams and checklists
- Customer feedback loops and NPS surveys
- Performance analytics dashboards
- Mystery shoppers or internal audits

Jay T Solutions once delayed a major product release by three weeks because it failed our internal quality benchmark. We took the short-term loss for long-term trust. That's how brands become legends.

Principle: Never let volume drown your voice.

8. **Invest in Scalable Infrastructure**

   Scaling on shaky infrastructure is like building skyscrapers on sand.

Your technology, logistics, and back-office systems must support your growth goals.

Consider:

- Cloud-based infrastructure for remote teams

- Scalable e-commerce and payment gateways

- Modular inventory and supply chain systems

- Legal, tax, and compliance structures across regions

Lesson: Infrastructure is not an expense—it's a growth multiplier.

9. **Monitor the Right Metrics**

   You can't scale what you don't measure. Tracking the right numbers allows you to make strategic decisions without guessing.

Essential metrics:

- Customer acquisition cost (CAC)

- Customer lifetime value (CLTV)

- Churn rate

- Gross margin

- Time to fulfil/deliver

- Team productivity KPIs

- Brand reputation scores

Remember: what you measure reveals what you value. Ensure your KPIs align with your vision and values.

10. **Scale Vision, Not Just Operations**

    Lastly, don't just scale the "how." Scale the "why."

Your business should grow not just in transaction, but in transformation.

Ask yourself:

- Is our impact growing with our revenue?
- Are we solving deeper problems or just selling more products?
- Are we inspiring more people, communities, and industries?

When I began writing books like The Mind of a Trillionaire and The DNA of Financial Greatness, it wasn't to build a bigger brand—it was to scale possibility. My words went places I never could. That's true scalability.

Final Thought:

"Scale is not an escape from the garage. It is a deepening of the dream. And dreams deserve structure, systems, and soul."

– Justine Ehiwario

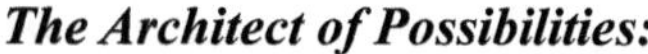

Justine Ehiwario

Chapter 12:

Weathering the Storm: How Visionaries Navigate Crisis, Competition, and Change

"It is not the strongest of the species that survives, nor the most intelligent. It is the one most adaptable to change."
— Charles Darwin

"Storms don't break visionaries. They refine them."
— Justine Ehiwario, The Things Wealthy People Do

INTRODUCTION: THE STORM IS NOT AN INTERRUPTION—IT IS A TEACHER.

Every great business and every bold visionary will, at some point, face storms. These are not minor disruptions or temporary inconveniences. They are existential tests—economic meltdowns, technological shifts, market crashes, political upheaval, brand scandals, pandemics, betrayals, or personal health crises.

In every industry—from engineering to fashion, real estate to technology—storms are not the exception; they are part of the terrain.

As I wrote in The Mind of a Trillionaire, "Visionaries do not ask for easier roads. They ask for stronger legs."

This chapter explores the mindset, strategies, and systems that allow architects of possibility to stand firm—and even rise stronger—when everything around them is shaking.

1. **EMBRACE THE STORM AS A CRUCIBLE, NOT A CURSE**

   Most people fear crisis. Visionaries leverage it.

The truth is, pressure reveals priorities. Storms show you what in your business is truly essential, and what is fluff. They spotlight the cracks in your systems, the weaknesses in your culture, the gaps in your leadership.

When a crisis hits, ask:

- What assumptions no longer hold true?
- What core values will I double down on?
- What opportunities does this unlock that stability blinded me from?

Pain is a signal. Possibility is a response.

2. **DEVELOP ANTIFRAGILE BUSINESS MODELS**

   In The DNA of Financial Greatness, I outlined the concept of antifragility—systems that don't just survive shocks but grow stronger because of them.

Here's how to build antifragility into your enterprise:

- Diversify income streams (don't depend on a single customer or market)
- Build remote-friendly operations
- Reduce fixed costs and increase variable, scalable partnerships
- Invest in cash reserves or emergency funds
- Train cross-functional teams so roles are fluid, not rigid

Resilience is enduring pressure. Antifragility is harnessing it.

3. **CULTIVATE CRISIS-READY LEADERSHIP**
   A storm reveals whether you're a captain or just a passenger. As a founder or executive, your ability to communicate clearly, act decisively, and remain emotionally anchored becomes the bedrock others cling to.

Essentials of visionary leadership in crisis:

- Tell the truth, fast. Don't spin—clarify.
- Over communicate internally and externally.
- Make high-quality decisions under pressure.
- Lean on advisors but trust your convictions.
- Stay visible, even if afraid. Presence creates stability.

4. **TURN COMPETITION INTO CATALYST**
   Competition intensifies during storms as resources shrink and

attention becomes scarce. Instead of fighting the competition, learn from it.

Ask:

- What are our competitors doing better?
- What are they missing that we can own?
- How can we turn their strength into our niche?

Consider how JAY T CLOTHING differentiated from mass-production apparel brands. Instead of competing on price, we competed on uniqueness, creativity, and customized family-centred designs. While others raced to the bottom, we climbed to distinction.

Your edge often hides in your enemy's blind spot.

5. **INNOVATE UNDER PRESSURE**

   Crisis compresses time. What would normally take a year must now happen in a week. Pressure is not the enemy of innovation—it is the accelerator.

Here's how visionaries innovate during turmoil:

- Launch MVPs (Minimum Viable Products) fast
- Use customer feedback loops for real-time refinement
- Reallocate team energy toward solving the new problems
- Reinvent your business model or pricing structure
- Experiment, test, and learn without shame

In the midst of market chaos, Jay T Solutions: Engineering Services launched a rapid prototype program for small infrastructure firms. What began as a three-month survival plan became a long-term revenue stream.

Necessity doesn't just birth invention—it demands it.

6. **MAINTAIN THE MISSION, FLEX THE METHOD**
   Your "why" must remain unshaken. Your "how" must remain fluid.

Storms destroy businesses that cling to outdated methods. They sharpen those who remain committed to impact but flexible on execution.

For example:

- The mission of Jay T Luxury Homes is to elevate the lifestyle of elite clients through bespoke design. Whether that's achieved via virtual tours, international collaborations, or local artisan partnerships is subject to change.
- The mission of Justech International is to simplify digital complexity. Whether that's through app development, SaaS tools, or remote IT support may evolve.

As I often say: Principles are anchors. Strategies are sails.

7. **LEVERAGE COMMUNITY, PARTNERSHIPS, AND TRUST**

   No visionary survives in isolation. During crisis, your ecosystem becomes your lifeline.

Build partnerships:

- Collaborate with aligned brands for cross-promotion
- Lean into your mentor and investor networks
- Offer mutual aid with businesses in complementary fields
- Build or join mastermind groups for emotional resilience and strategic thinking

In crisis, collaboration is currency.

8. **REBOUND STRONGER: POST-CRISIS GROWTH STRATEGY**

   The best leaders don't just survive storms—they learn from them and adapt for the future.

Post-crisis, conduct a "lessons audit":

- What failed—and why?
- What saved us—and how?
- What systems should be upgraded?
- What new markets or needs were revealed?

Design a post-crisis action plan that includes:

- Upgrading your infrastructure and tools
- Diversifying suppliers and revenue models
- Retraining staff for broader roles
- Communicating lessons transparently with stakeholders

9. INTERNAL RESILIENCE: THE SOUL OF THE VISIONARY

Ultimately, it's not just systems, strategies, or teams that weather storms—it's your spirit.

Build habits of emotional resilience:

- Journal your thoughts daily
- Exercise and nourish your body
- Take Sabbath rest—burnout doesn't build legends
- Surround yourself with thinkers, not just doers
- Remember why you started

Your mind is your greatest asset in a storm. Guard it fiercely.

FINAL THOUGHT

"You can't stop the wind, but you can build a better sail. You can't stop the rain, but you can build stronger shelter. Storms don't last forever—but visionaries do."

— Justine Ehiwario

Chapter 13:

Funding the Future: Visionary Capital Strategies for Long-Term Growth

"In business, money is not just capital—it is fuel for vision, a bridge between the idea and its global impact."
— Justine Ehiwario, The Unstoppable Road to Wealth Creation

"Capital goes where it is respected and multiplies where it is wisely deployed."
— Warren Buffett

Introduction: Vision Without Capital Is a Dream Deferred

Every revolutionary enterprise requires more than imagination and hustle. It demands funding. Without capital, even the boldest idea remains grounded. But visionary entrepreneurs do not just chase money—they attract it strategically, wield it wisely, and multiply it deliberately.

Funding the future is not merely about raising rounds of investment. It's about designing capital strategies aligned with your mission, stage, and scale. It's about understanding when to bootstrap and when to seek partners. When to conserve and when to accelerate.

This final chapter will unpack the key funding philosophies, practical tools, and long-term growth tactics used by today's most effective entrepreneurial architects. Whether you're building a global tech company, a socially impactful brand, or a multi-sector empire like Jay T Solutions Ltd, your mastery of visionary capital will define your legacy.

1. The Funding Mindset: Shift from Scarcity to Strategy

Money doesn't follow need; it follows clarity, confidence, and competency.

Too many founders operate from desperation—begging for loans or investors without a value proposition. Instead, adopt a capital-conscious mindset:

- Funding is a tool, not a goal.
- Equity is precious—don't give it away cheaply.
- Not all money is smart money.
- Vision creates attraction; execution sustains confidence.

In my book The Things Wealthy People Do, I shared how capital naturally gravitates to those with structure, proof, and a compelling story. Investors, banks, and customers want to know: "Can you deliver?"

Start thinking like a fund manager: how will every dollar invested generate exponential returns—financially, socially, and strategically?

2. Bootstrapping Brilliance: Building Without Big Capital

Most iconic companies didn't start with millions—they started lean.

Bootstrapping means building your business using personal savings, customer revenue, or reinvested profits instead of outside investors. It's about staying scrappy, self-reliant, and efficient.

Benefits of bootstrapping:

- Full ownership and control
- Encourages disciplined growth
- Forces product-market fit quickly
- Builds resilience

JAY T CLOTHING, for example, began with heat transfers and hand-finished T-shirts using basic equipment. Today, it's a global fashion identity operating on multiple marketplaces—all from strategic reinvestment and relentless execution.

Bootstrapping isn't poverty—it's training for mastery.

3. Strategic Capital: Know When to Raise, Who to Raise From

There comes a time when capital acceleration is necessary—for hiring, scaling, entering new markets, or investing in infrastructure.

But not all capital is equal.

Here are key funding options:

- **Friends and Family:** useful at idea stage, high trust
- **Angel Investors:** ideal for early-stage experimentation
- **Venture Capital:** high-risk, high-return investors; come with expectations
- **Private Equity:** for mature companies with stable cash flows
- **Bank Loans:** predictable repayment, retain full ownership
- **Government Grants:** often non-dilutive and sector-specific
- **Crowdfunding:** builds community and capital simultaneously

At Justech International, we delayed external capital until we had proven systems and recurring clients. When we finally accepted private equity funding, we were able to scale development teams, launch mobile solutions, and automate customer service—all without sacrificing vision.

The right capital partner should bring more than money—they should bring mentorship, market access, or momentum.

4. Protecting Your Equity: Ownership Is Leverage

Ownership is one of the most undervalued assets by early entrepreneurs.

Giving away 30% of your company at the idea stage can cost you millions later. Be intentional:

- Keep early rounds small and smart
- Use convertible notes or SAFE agreements to delay valuation
- Explore revenue-based financing models
- Offer performance-based equity to early team members
- Use phantom equity for advisors or key contractors

Always ask: Will this deal help us grow sustainably, or am I trading long-term value for short-term survival?

In Jay T Prime Properties, we retained full family ownership until we reached profitability. Today, we leverage equity selectively for large-scale developments, but our autonomy is our strength.

5. Build for Profitability from Day One

Venture capital culture has glamorized growth at all costs. But in the real world, profit is freedom.

A visionary company:

- Designs its pricing model to sustain and grow
- Builds repeatable revenue engines
- Identifies high-margin products or services early
- Manages operational expenses proactively
- Avoids over-hiring before product-market fit

In The DNA of Financial Greatness, I emphasized the power of building a business that funds itself. When you're profitable, you choose your destiny. You don't chase investors—you choose them.

As I often teach: Revenue is vanity. Profit is sanity. Cash flow is sovereignty.

6. Scaling with Systems, Not Just Spending

Funding doesn't fix broken systems—it amplifies them.

Before pouring in capital, visionary entrepreneurs build:

- Clear SOPs (standard operating procedures)
- Automation pipelines for marketing, sales, and fulfilment
- Delegation structures and reporting lines
- Scalable customer support and CRM tools
- Measurable KPIs and dashboards

At Jay T Solutions: Engineering Services, we delayed hiring until our operational backend could handle project loads predictably. By investing in systems first, our scalability became sustainable—not chaotic.

Money multiplies systems. Without systems, it evaporates.

7. Think Generationally: Legacy Capital Strategies

Wealth isn't just built—it's transferred. If you want to become the architect of not just a business, but a dynasty, think long term.

Visionary legacy strategies include:

- Trusts and family offices to manage assets

- Real estate holdings for long-term cash flow
- Business succession planning
- Strategic partnerships with family or protégés
- Multi-country incorporation for tax optimization

Justine Ehiwario's family of businesses—from fashion to engineering to real estate—operates under a parent company with strategic succession plans and interlocking value chains.

Legacy isn't about ego. It's about continuity.

Final Reflections: Capital Is Not Just About Money—It's About Mission

As you close this book, remember:

Capital is not the destination. It is a tool to manifest your mission. It is the breath that gives life to your blueprint. It is the scaffolding that holds your ideas above the noise.

But more than funding, you are the most valuable asset.

Your mindset. Your vision. Your resilience. Your ability to believe when the world doubts. To build when others retreat. To sow when others consume.

You are the architect of possibilities.

Let this be your charge: Build with courage. Lead with integrity. Fund with wisdom. Grow with love. Scale with soul.

Because the world doesn't need more businesses.

It needs more visionary builders like you.

The End!

Epilogue:

The Legacy of the Builder

Every generation is shaped by those bold enough to imagine what doesn't yet exist—and build it anyway.

Throughout history, it has never been the conformists who left an enduring mark. It has always been the visionaries, the misfits, the rebels, the dreamers, and the doers. The entrepreneurs who looked at chaos and saw patterns. The builders who stared into uncertainty and laid foundations. The architects who saw not what is, but what could be—and took action to bring it into reality.

You, the reader of this book, are that kind of person.

Whether you are just launching your idea, expanding your enterprise, or transforming your industry, this book has served as a blueprint, a compass, and a call to greatness.

But now, the pages end. The responsibility begins.

Your mission is not to memorize principles but to embody them. Not to merely absorb wisdom—but to activate it. Not to follow the crowd—but to blaze the trail.

Let your company reflect your convictions.

Let your leadership echo your values.

Let your vision uplift others—communities, nations, generations.

Because the future is not inherited. It is architected.

And the world is waiting for what only you can build.

Acknowledgments

I am deeply grateful for the divine inspiration and purpose that have fueled my journey. To God be the glory.

To my beloved wife, Odion—you are the heartbeat of my vision and the pillar of our family. Your wisdom, patience, and strength continue to inspire me every day. To our children—Justine, Jason, and Jolene—you are the legacy I build for and with. May you always dream bold, build strong, and live with purpose.

To my closest brother, Michael—your belief in me and our shared values have been a source of strength.

To the teams behind Jay T Solutions, Jay T Prime Properties, Jay T Luxury Homes, Jay T Solutions Engineering Services, and Justech International—thank you for embodying the spirit of excellence, loyalty, and innovation. Together, we've proven that vision has no limits.

To my readers—your hunger for growth and transformation is the reason I write. May every word in this book serve as a seed that yields greatness in your life and business.

Finally, to the pioneers, mentors, authors, and entrepreneurs—past and present—who laid the intellectual and industrial foundation upon which we stand: thank you for being beacons of possibility.

www.ingramcontent.com/pod-product-compliance
Lightning Source LLC
LaVergne TN
LVHW010346200726
843507LV00010B/1667